Not by Bread

Daily Reflections for Lent 2013

Bishop Robert F. Morneau

LITURGICAL PRESS

Collegeville, Minnesota

www.litpress.org

ISSN: 1550-803X

ISBN: 978-0-8146-3453-0

Introduction

The word "Lent" connotes, for many of us, a season of prayer and penance. And so it is. But the etymology of Lent is grounded in "springtime." Our eyes are set on the great Easter mystery, the gift of life and light as nature celebrates its rebirth.

Seed companies are busy sending out their products of all varieties: cucumbers, carrots, squash, pumpkins, watermelon, etc. Gardeners will gently set them in the dark, dank earth, a tomb if you will. Within days (weeks) tiny plants will emerge as if rising from the dead. Spring is the season of the paschal mystery made visible. All of Lent is a season of dying and rising.

Might there be a game plan for this liturgical season, a game plan similar to the sporting world? Are there words of advice that might enrich our pilgrim journey as disciples of Jesus? Here are several suggestions.

Ne quid nimis ("Less rather than more"). Our culture models for us self-indulgence. We eat and drink more than we need; we think our wants are needs; we fail to distinguish between what is essential and unnecessary. By paring back, space is created for the invasion of grace. Wherever God finds emptiness and hospitality, divine grace will flood our souls. Asceticism's main goal is not self-denial but opening ourselves to God's will. Thus, "less rather than more" has spiritual significance.

Age quod agis ("Do what you are doing"). John Henry Cardinal Newman maintained that our growth in holiness consists in doing our daily duties well, be it changing diapers, building roads, teaching a class, doing the works of mercy. The road to holiness is to do, in the here and now, what God is asking of us in our own unique circumstances. On the reverse side of this spirituality is the acceptance of what comes our way, be it joys or sorrows, delights or burdens. This "passive fidelity" was lived so powerfully by Blessed Mother Teresa of Calcutta, who continually reminded her sisters to give what God takes and to take what God gives.

In omnibus respice finem ("In all things look to the end"). Just as coaches look for the conference championship, and base all of their training and decisions on this goal, so disciples of Jesus look to the goal of full participation in the life of Jesus—his life, death, and resurrection. By so doing we unite ourselves with God and find union with one another. This oneness was the end that Jesus prayed for in the Gospel of John. Lent is about discipleship and keeping our eye on the goal of eternal life.

Quidquid recipitur ad modum recipientis recipitur ("Whatever is received is received according to the mode of the receiver"). Disposition is determinative. Rain in the desert causes a flash flood. The ground is hard and baked, unable to absorb the downpour. Our souls need to be receptive to the grace of God's word and sacrament if spiritual growth is to occur. Such dispositions as hospitality, affability, and gentleness prepare the soul for the seeds of new life.

"Love and do what you will" (St. Augustine). Always the bottom line is love, being loved by God and giving that love away. The great Pauline hymn from 1 Corinthians says it all: no love and we are nothing, even if we give everything away and offer our bodies to be burned. Lent is a season of love, love for God, love for the needy, love for all creation. When love is authentic, we will do nothing wrong. Concern, respect, and responsibility will characterize our lives.

The journey of Lent is focused on participating more deeply in the life of Christ. Having a game plan might well foster that participation.

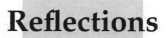

Reflections

Your Whole Heart

Readings: Joel 2:12-18; 2 Cor 5:20–6:2; Matt 6:1-6, 16-18

Scripture:
Even now, says the LORD,
    return to me with your whole heart,
    with fasting, and weeping, and mourning;
Rend your hearts, not your garments,
    and return to the LORD, your God. (Joel 2:12-13a)

Reflection: Lent is a season of conversion, a turning, a returning to the God revealed in Jesus, a God who is gracious, merciful, and rich in kindness. Often we stray from the center of our being, getting caught up in distractions that divide our hearts and souls. Like the lost sheep in the gospel, we drift from the fold and, in our loneliness, hear the call to come home.

Joel the prophet passes on God's message: return to the Lord with your whole heart. We do that by putting into practice the three imperatives of today's gospel: pray, fast, give alms. In prayer we lift our minds and hearts to a God who is slow to anger and relenting in punishment. By fasting, we train our wills to do the will of God. And, by almsgiving, we reach out to those in need through financial assistance and social service. It is not sufficient just to *do* these things; we must *do* them in a certain way—wholeheartedly.

As the ashes are placed on our foreheads we are told, "Turn away from sin and be faithful to the Gospel" (Mark 1:15). This turning and this fidelity are primarily the work of the Holy Spirit. True, we must cooperate on this spiritual journey but the initiative is always with God. Saint Paul was well aware of this in his own conversion story. On that road to Damascus, Paul (then Saul) was turned around and invited into the life of Jesus. Years later he would write to the Corinthians (and to us), "We implore you on behalf of Christ, be reconciled to God" (2 Cor 5:20b). Paul was one who returned to God with all his heart, unreservedly.

Meditation: What types of activities do you undertake that engage your whole heart? Of the three Lenten imperatives—pray, fast, give alms—which one do you feel is especially important for you? What will be your response?

Prayer: Gracious and merciful Lord, as we begin this holy season of Lent, send your Spirit of fidelity and hope into our hearts. Too often our hearts are divided, our minds are distracted. Help us to focus on doing your will and building your kingdom. May this season of Lent help us to grow in our discipleship.

Making a Difference

Readings: Deut 30:15-20; Luke 9:22-25

Scripture:
Moses said to the people:
  "Today I have set before you
  life and prosperity, death and doom.
If you obey the commandments of the LORD . . .
  you will live and grow numerous . . ." (Deut 30:15, 16b)

Reflection: Robert Frost's poem "The Road Not Taken" is well known. The poet tells of two roads that a traveler comes across and a decision must be made as to which one will be taken. Should one go to the right or to the left; should one take the well-worn road or the less traveled one? This poem captures the option that Moses presented to the people of his day: the road of life or death, the road of prosperity or doom. That choice will make a radical difference, determining one's destiny and changing history.

In 2010, LIFE Books published *100 People Who Changed the World*. The list included religious figures, philosophers, political leaders, scientists, inventors, and cultural icons. On the cover of the publication are photos of Jesus, Lincoln, Oprah, Gandhi, Beethoven, Martin Luther King, Mother Teresa of Calcutta, Adolf Hitler, Nelson Mandela, and the Beatles. Whether for good or ill, these individuals changed history because they exercised their freedom in choosing a road to travel.

Jesus chose the road of obedience. His focus was always on doing the Father's will and bringing about the kingdom, God's reign in the human heart and in history. That obedience would involve suffering; that obedience would lead to peace. This is the road that Jesus presents to us this Lent: the royal road of obedience. Essentially, this is the call to discipleship. By losing our life, we save it. This great paradox can be lived only through God's grace.

There is a background song for the Lenten season: "Go Make a Difference." Indeed, we can make a difference when guided and empowered by the Holy Spirit.

Meditation: What road are you walking? In what ways are you changing history?

Prayer: Lord Jesus, you invite us to journey with you on the royal road of obedience. Help us to focus on the Father's will; help us to exercise our freedom with graced responsibility. Our lives will make a difference, for good or ill. Send your Spirit to show us the way, the way of love and compassion and forgiveness.

Curious Fascination

Readings: Isa 58:1-9a; Matt 9:14-15

Scripture:
Your vindication shall go before you,
 and the glory of the LORD shall be your rear guard.
Then you shall call, and the LORD will answer,
 you shall cry for help, and he will say: Here I am!
 (Isa 58:8b-9)

Reflection: William James (1842–1910), the noted American psychologist/philosopher, made an interesting observation in his book *Pragmatism*: "There is, it must be confessed, a curious fascination in having deep things talked about, even though neither we nor the disputants understand them."

During this season of Lent, we speak about many deep things: the paschal mystery, the suffering of our incarnate God, the call to conversion, the nature of sin and grace, the enigma of the cross, the glory of the resurrection. Deep things, indeed, are difficult to fathom and comprehend. Yet, we must speak about them because they are the core of our faith life.

Today the liturgy talks about fasting. Do we truly understand what this spiritual discipline is all about? Isaiah attempts to clarify it for us. The type of asceticism that God is asking from us is not about sackcloth and ashes, not about bowing our heads like reeds in the wind. No, God wants us to reach out to those in need, to free the oppressed, to provide shelter for the homeless. This is the fasting God desires.

Another "deep thing" is talked about in the gospel. It's about the presence of someone who is very important (here, the bridegroom) and the question is, how are we to respond to that presence? Jesus is clear: no mourning or fasting when the bridegroom is present. Rather, we are to rejoice and celebrate.

It is fascinating that, though we cannot fathom the depth of deep things, we are curious about them. Lent's deepest "thing" is Jesus, our Brother, Friend, Redeemer. Through prayer and reflection, we might come to deeper knowledge of this beloved Bridegroom.

Meditation: What "deep things" in your life cause curious fascination? What is your understanding of the nature of fasting and asceticism in the Christian life?

Prayer: Lord Jesus, teach us to ponder the "deep things" of life. Too often we are distracted by superficial entertainment and waste our time on inane matters. Send your Spirit of wisdom into our hearts so that we might come to know and love you and your Father.

The Divine Physician

Readings: Isa 58:9b-14; Luke 5:27-32

Scripture:
The Pharisees and their scribes complained to his
    disciples, saying,
  "Why do you eat and drink with tax collectors and
    sinners?" (Luke 5:30)

Reflection: Father Karl Rahner (1904–84), one of the most brilliant theologians of the twentieth century, wrote extensively on the mystery of the Trinity. He spoke of the "immanent Trinity," the very inner life of God, and the "economic Trinity," the activity of God. It is through what God "does" that we come to know who God "is."

For Christians, Jesus is the central revelation of the very mystery of God. Jesus is constantly teaching in synagogues and on mountainsides, proclaiming the kingdom of God, and curing those who are ill, be it of body, mind, or spirit. Through his redemptive work, Jesus calls sinners to repentance and offers them the peace that is far beyond our understanding. Jesus is our Redeemer, our Divine Physician.

Isaiah, in our first reading, speaks about the "repairer of the breach" and "restorer of ruined homesteads." When we follow Jesus in authentic discipleship, we are called to repair what is broken and restore to wholeness that which is injured. Surely Matthew felt that call as he followed Jesus; surely Matthew, a tax collector and friend of sinners, knew that all righteousness was grounded in faith.

In the Eucharist, Jesus comes to eat and drink with saints and sinners, with the righteous and the unrighteous, with you and me. For that table fellowship, we give thanks; for that table fellowship, we experience the very life of God, be it immanent or economical.

Meditation: What have you repaired or restored in your life and in the life of others? How do you grow in your knowledge of God? Is the mystery of creation or the mystery of redemption more revelatory of God for you?

Prayer: Triune God, our limited intelligence struggles to know you, the source of all life and holiness. Send your Spirit of knowledge into our hearts so that we might come to know the mystery of your love revealed in Jesus, the Divine Physician. Send your Spirit of courage so that we might truly follow your way.

The River and the Desert

Readings: Deut 26:4-10; Rom 10:8-13; Luke 4:1-13

Scripture:
Filled with the Holy Spirit, Jesus returned from the Jordan
and was led by the Spirit into the desert for forty days,
to be tempted by the devil. (Luke 4:1-2a)

Reflection: The river and the desert are images that touch
the depth of our humanity. Water is the source of life; barren
wilderness speaks of the silence and solitude that forces us
to look deeply into reality. The great spiritual writers of all
traditions have had much to say about deserts and rivers.
Poets and philosophers too.

Jesus knew both terrains. At the Jordan River he was baptized and experienced the power of the Holy Spirit. Hearing
himself addressed as the Beloved, as the Son of God, was a
crossroads experience. In his passion, as he hung upon the
cross, Jesus' crossroad experience would be challenged as
the taunting began: "If you are the Son of God, . . ." Deep
in his memory were etched the Jordan words that would
sustain him in the hour of darkness.

In the desert, our Lord came into contact with those forces
that would separate him from his Father. Jesus was tempted
to embrace the three idols that are common to every culture
and time: power, prestige, and possessions. Jesus would have

none of it. Obedience defined his life and he would do only what the Father asked of him. In that barren desert, in that apparent waste and loneliness, Jesus remained faithful.

Rivers speak of life. Jesus' mission was to give life, life to the full (John 10:10). As baptized Christians we too are called to be agents of life. The water poured out in the sacrament of initiation is not meant just for us. Rather, the life given to us is to be shared with others. The temptation here is to hoard, to keep to ourselves what has been given. Disciples see themselves as a conduit of God's life; Christian stewards know that their call is to receive God's gifts gratefully and to share those gifts sacrificially.

Deserts speak of trials and ordeals. Life is messy. Everywhere we turn there is suffering—poor health, broken relationships, abuse, wars, corruption. A huge temptation is to become sour and to view life from a negative perspective. Our great need is the gift of the Holy Spirit, the same Spirit that sustained Jesus in his trials. A contemporary mentor for us here is Blessed Mother Teresa of Calcutta, who, for many years, experienced the desolation of the desert. Out of that poverty and pain she bore witness to God's compassion by her unselfish love.

Meditation: What do rivers and deserts symbolize for you? What are the temptations that hinder your spiritual growth?

Prayer: Lord Jesus, be with us as we journey along riverbanks and barren deserts. We hunger for life and love; we face the trials of desolation and despair. Send your Spirit into our hearts and make us authentic disciples.

The Holiness of God

Readings: Lev 19:1-2, 11-18; Matt 25:31-46

Scripture:
The LORD said to Moses,
  "Speak to the whole assembly of the children of Israel
    and tell them:
  Be holy, for I, the LORD, your God, am holy." (Lev 19:1-2)

Reflection: Holiness is more than doing; holiness is a matter of being. The saints are holy because their minds and hearts are conformed to the image of God, a God of love. Holiness is the perfection of love and that love will be expressed by keeping the commandments and doing the works of mercy.

In his scholarly work *Asking the Fathers*, Aelred Squire argues that holiness is grounded in fidelity to God's will. Then he distinguishes two ways of being faithful, one active, the other passive. Active fidelity lies in doing the obligations that come with our state in life. For teachers, that means being prepared as one enters the classroom. For doctors, it means being competent in one's field of medicine. For engineers, it is building highways and skyscrapers according to the blueprint. Holiness is doing what our vocation calls us to be.

The other manner of holiness is in the realm of passivity. Things happen to us, be it suffering or loss. By embracing what comes without resentment and anger, we grow in holiness. This "passive fidelity" is the other side of the coin and often much harder to bear.

To love is to become Godlike. To be an agent of light is to become Godlike. To give life to others is to become Godlike. In the Eucharist, we cry out, "Holy! Holy! Holy!" We do that in response to God's love, light, and life. And then, after receiving Jesus, the fountain and source of holiness, we venture forth into the mission field as instruments of God's love, light, and life. And, marvelous to behold, the exclamation of holy, holy, holy becomes glory, glory, glory. For when we are conformed to the holiness of God, we radiate God's glory.

Meditation: What is your understanding of holiness? Who are the holy people in your life? How do they radiate God's glory?

Prayer: Holy God, we do praise your name for your name is Love and Mercy. Give us the vision to see your glory; give us the courage to live your life. Draw us beyond ourselves into the circle of your providential compassion. Make us radiate your peace and joy.

God's Effective Word

Readings: Isa 55:10-11; Matt 6:7-15

Scripture:
Thus says the LORD: . . .
So shall my word be
    that goes forth from my mouth;
It shall not return to me void,
    but shall do my will,
    achieving the end for which I sent it. (Isa 55:10a-11)

Reflection: Back in 1989, Stephen R. Covey wrote *7 Habits of Highly Effective People: Restoring the Character Ethic*. Over fifteen million copies have been sold. Obviously, not only does Covey write about effectiveness but his writing is itself effective as individuals and businesses have been transformed by living the seven habits Covey articulates.

God's word is effective, that is, it accomplishes the task it was sent to do. This is especially true of *the* Word, Jesus, who came among us for our redemption. Jesus did the Father's will through his obedience and fidelity. And Jesus has left us a number of words that, like the rain and snow, must not return void.

Pray! Not only is the imperative given that we are to pray but Jesus also gives us the text of the great prayer, the Our Father. With utter simplicity and directness, we ask that

God's name be reverenced, that God's will be done, that God's kingdom might come. We ask for our daily bread, for forgiveness, for deliverance from evil and temptation. We have here both clarity and profundity. No babble, just heart speaking to heart.

Justice! In the communion antiphon we pray, "My God of justice, you answer my cry; you come to my help when I am in trouble. Take pity on me, Lord, and hear my prayer" (Ps 4:2). God is concerned with right relationship, and for relationships to be correct, justice must be done. Rights must be respected; duties must be fulfilled.

Compassion! Jesus, the Word, impels us to be as compassionate as his Father is. This compassion will be effective to the extent that we crawl inside the skin of other people and know what they are truly experiencing.

Meditation: What word has God given to you? How effective are the words you speak, be it in prayer or daily conversation? What habits shape your spiritual life?

Prayer: Word of God, dwell deep within our hearts. Open our ears to the sound of your voice; give us the strength to do what you ask. Come, Holy Spirit, come.

The Lord's Bidding

Readings: Jonah 3:1-10; Luke 11:29-32

Scripture:
"Set out for the great city of Nineveh,
and announce to it the message that I will tell you."
So Jonah made ready and went to Nineveh,
according to the LORD's bidding. (Jonah 3:2-3a)

Reflection: At the center of our spiritual life is the discernment question. What is the bidding of the Lord? What is God asking us to do in our times, in our culture? Jonah heard God's voice and went to Nineveh, where he did God's bidding.

Jesus makes reference in the gospel today to Jonah, the queen of the south, and the wisdom of Solomon. Jesus is challenging his generation (and ours) to respond to God's will. He himself is the standard for all discernment; Jesus himself is the obedient, compassionate, and loving one.

So what is discernment all about? It is a sorting out process by which we, in faith, interpret life experience from God's point of view. Discernment is figuring out which of the impulses, whispers, nudges, proddings, and BIDDINGS are from God and which are not. Ultimately we know by consequences: Do these biddings lead to union with God and unity in the human family or not? Do these biddings result in love, joy, and peace?

But it is not all that simple. So many voices seek our attention; so many impulses and nudges are complex; so many regrets and worries obscure our thinking. Our prayer must be, "Come, Holy Spirit, come." We must beg for the gift of discernment as well as for the gift of courage to act on our clarities. It is one thing to know what God is asking; it is another to do it.

Blessed Mother Teresa of Calcutta had to discern a call within a call. She left one community to form a new one. No easy process, this! But she did God's bidding and the world is a different place.

Meditation: What do you understand by discernment? What nudges and biddings has the Lord given you this Lent?

Prayer: Lord God, as you bid Jonah to call the people of Nineveh to repentance, you bid us in our times to turn away from sin and believe in the gospel. May we hear your voice and do your will. Come, Lord Jesus, come.

Asking, Seeking, Knocking

Readings: Esth C:12, 14-16, 23-25; Matt 7:7-12

Scripture:
Jesus said to his disciples:
   "Ask and it will be given to you;
   seek and you will find;
   knock and the door will be opened to you." (Matt 7:7)

Reflection: Queen Esther, in our first reading, asked for the Lord's help, she who was alone and frightened. More, she asked that mourning be turned into gladness, that sorrow be turned into wholeness. The Lord heard her request and answered her.

In the verse before the gospel we pray, "A clean heart create for me, God; / give me back the joy of your salvation." All of us, in our own unique ways, seek salvation, that oneness with God and one another. Seeking joy and peace is at the heart of discipleship.

And knocking is the third imperative. The psalmist prays, "Lord, on the day I called for help, you answered me" (Ps 138:3a). In our responsorial refrain we knock at the door of God's heart and the Lord is attentive to the cry of the poor, we his people.

Asking! Seeking! Knocking! Receiving! Finding! Opening! Our providential God gives us what we need. Sometimes it is not what we ask for; sometimes it is not what we seek; sometimes certain doors are not opened because that opening would not serve us well. God's ways are different from our own, but we can be assured that God has our best interests at heart. The good gifts that God bestows are those of life and love. These are the graces that matter. If we ask for trivial things, God in his wisdom will withhold them from us lest they cause us to wander from him.

In his poem "The Pulley," George Herbert (1593–1633) describes how God bestows upon his creatures such gifts as beauty, wisdom, honor, and pleasure. But then God did not give us the gift of rest lest we rest in God's gift and not the Giver. Such is God's wisdom. Our prayers are answered according to a larger plan than our own. Our asking, seeking, and knocking are responded to in the light of eternity.

Meditation: What are you currently seeking and asking for? What doors have been opened to you over the years? Do you believe in intercessory prayer?

Prayer: God of wisdom and love, hear our prayers for help. Give us what we need, not what we want. Deepen our faith in your divine providence and fill us with trust. You are a loving Father who knows what is best for us.

Peter's Gifts

Readings: 1 Pet 5:1-4; Matt 16:13-19

Scripture:
Tend the flock of God in your midst,
　　overseeing not by constraint but willingly,
　　as God would have it, not for shameful profit but
　　　　eagerly.
Do not lord it over those assigned to you,
　　but be examples to the flock. (1 Pet 5:2-3)

Reflection: The influential spiritual writer Thomas Merton (1915–68), in one of his many letters, speaks about three gifts that God gave to him: his Catholic faith, his monastic vocation (Trappist monk at Gethsemani), and his vocation as a writer. These three blessings gave Merton a center around which the rest of his life found meaning.

The influential apostle Peter also had his gifts: his deep faith in Jesus, his openness to God's word, and his leadership.

Simon Peter proclaimed Jesus as the Anointed One, the Son of God. This faith was a gift, one that enabled Peter to see beyond appearances into the heart of mystery. While not understanding the full depth of the person of Jesus, Peter was given enough insight to recognize the son of Mary as the Messiah. Here is the one who would save the world and offer the possibility of peace.

Simon Peter was open to God's word. Although others listened to the crowds and guessed that Jesus might be John the Baptist or Elijah or Jeremiah, Peter listened to the inner voice, God's word of revelation. What was manifest in Caesarea Philippi, the fountainhead of the Jordan River, was the eternal Son of God. This revelation changed Peter's life and the very life of the world.

Simon Peter was called to lead. As the Vicar of Christ, he would be given keys, the power to open and close. This power and authority was to be put at the service of others. No lording it over anyone. This servant leadership was for the building up of the church, the Body of Christ. This leadership was given for the sake of the kingdom.

Meditation: How has God gifted you? In what ways do those gifts further the kingdom and build up the Mystical Body of Christ?

Prayer: Saint Peter, pray for us. Help us discern God's call; help us to name and actualize our gifts. May we, like you, recognize Jesus, the Anointed One. May we, like you, be open to God's living word.

Walking in God's Way

Readings: Deut 26:16-19; Matt 5:43-48

Scripture:
Moses spoke to the people, saying: . . .
"Today you are making this agreement with the LORD:
   he is to be your God and you are to walk in his ways
   and observe his statutes, commandments and decrees,
   and to hearken to his voice." (Deut 26:17)

Reflection: God has spoken about his ways not so much in words as in the person of *the* Word, Jesus. We are to hearken to his attitudes and behaviors, as well as to his teachings. If Jesus is our Master, if God is truly our God, then we live in a certain way.

Love your enemies. The Hindu Mohandas K. Gandhi (1869–1948), a spiritual and political leader from India, was deeply influenced by the New Testament, especially the Sermon on the Mount. In his teaching of nonviolence, Gandhi was presenting a way of dealing with one's enemies in a manner similar to the Scriptures. If we love those who hate us, we are living in accord with God's way.

Pray for those who persecute you. As Jesus hung upon the cross, he prayed for his persecutors. He asked the Father to forgive them and insisted that his persecutors did not know what they were doing. As disciples of the Lord, we made an agreement through our baptism and confirmation to emulate our Master. And it is because of the grace given in those sacraments and renewed time and time again in the Eucharist that we have the potential to do what Jesus did, that is, to pray for those who seek to injure or destroy us. Without that grace, such prayer is impossible.

Be perfect. As we read the lives of the saints, be it St. Augustine or St. Teresa of Avila, be it St. Monica or St. Paul, we see flawed human beings. Whether struggling with their sexuality or alcohol, arrogance or vanity, the saints lived in the human condition that is universal. Yet they strove for perfection, to walk the way of Jesus, the way of love and compassion and forgiveness. When they failed, they had the sacrament of reconciliation to restore and deepen their relationship with God.

Meditation: What agreements have you made with the Lord? How do you deal with your enemies and those who persecute you? What do you understand by "perfection"?

Prayer: Gracious God, guide us in your way. May we keep our eyes focused on Jesus, the compassionate and forgiving Lord. Grace us to forgive those who hurt us; grace us to ask forgiveness of those we have wounded. Renew your covenant with us today.

The Royal Road of Faith

Readings: Gen 15:5-12, 17-18; Phil 3:17–4:1; Luke 9:28b-36

Scripture:
The Lord God took Abram outside and said,
   "Look up at the sky and count the stars, if you can.
Just so," he added, "shall your descendants be."
Abram put his faith in the LORD,
   who credited it to him as an act of righteousness.
      (Gen 15:5-6)

Reflection: Faith is an endangered species in our times. The multiplicity of belief systems, the rampant relativism in the field of ethics, and the exclusion of God from the public square all lead to a deeper and deeper growth in secularism, a world that has no or little reference to God. Not surprisingly, drifting has become a pattern of so many. We have lost not just our moral compass but the spiritual GPS that gives us ultimate direction and meaning.

By contrast, we witness the faith of Abram, St. Paul, and Peter, James, and John.

Abram looked up into the starry, starry sky and was told by God that his descendants would be truly numerous. Abram believed! He put his trust in the word of God and it was credited to him as righteousness. Despite many obstacles, Abram relied on God's providential promise.

Saint Paul was a man of faith whose citizenship was with the saints in heaven. The Lord Jesus Christ and the mystery of the cross shaped Paul's thinking and acting. Paul's faith was expressed in zeal for the kingdom of God. It was a faith that became polemical when enemies of Jesus' cross led to immorality. Paul's faith was evangelical, calling the people of his day to embrace the way of love, compassion, and forgiveness.

Peter, James, and John had a faith experience that transformed their lives. In the mystery of the transfiguration they experienced Jesus as the one who fulfilled the law and the prophets, symbolized by Moses and Elijah. Their faith deepened when the voice from the cloud cried out, "This is my chosen Son; listen to him" (Luke 9:35b). Never again would they view Jesus in the same light; never again would they be able to forget the glory of the transfigured Christ.

The psalmist gives us a refrain to carry through the day, indeed, through our lives: "The LORD is my light and my salvation" (Ps 27:1a). If we believe that, we are on the royal road of faith.

Meditation: How has your faith grown in the last several years? What enhances and what diminishes your belief in the mystery of God? Who are your models of faith?

Prayer: Lord Jesus, may we listen to you as you speak to us through Abram, Paul, and the great apostles. Deepen our faith; deepen our love. So easily we slip off the royal road of faith into the ditch of doubt. Send your Spirit more deeply into our lives.

God's Merciful Covenant

Readings: Dan 9:4b-10; Luke 6:36-38

Scripture:
Jesus said to his disciples:
"Be merciful, just as your Father is merciful.

"Stop judging and you will not be judged.
Stop condemning and you will not be condemned.
Forgive and you will be forgiven." (Luke 6:36-38a)

Reflection: The prophet Daniel reminds us, "But yours, O Lord, our God, are compassion and forgiveness!" (Dan 9:9a). God is faithful to his "merciful covenant" and we are called to that same mercy, compassion, and forgiveness.

In Shakespeare's *The Merchant of Venice*, Portia offers these words of wisdom: "We do pray for mercy, / And that same prayer doth teach us all to render / The deeds of mercy." During this Lenten season we do well to pray for the gift of mercy. Honesty demands that we acknowledge and confess our sins; honesty calls us to humble repentance. But more is needed. Just as we ask to receive mercy, we are to pass that gift on to those who have in any way offended us. We are to forgive as we have been forgiven.

Jesus' imperatives are forceful as he calls us to be merciful, to stop judging and condemning, and to forgive. Here is a verse that one judge struggled with:

The Judge

Jesus said: "Stop judging!"

But I am a judge.
I have my bench and gavel,
I've been called to do justice.

Yet at night I keep hearing: "Stop judging!"
What am I to do
for is not God a judge
in whose image I have been made?

I know what I will do.
When I disrobe,
when I leave the bench,
I will kneel and repent.

Meditation: What "deeds of mercy" is God calling you to perform? Is there a difference between making a judgment and being judgmental?

Prayer: Lord Jesus, we pray for mercy and compassion. Without your grace, we will continue to be critical of others and unforgiving. Send your Spirit to transform our hearts, making them like your own. Help us to extend your covenant of mercy to all we meet.

Humility and Exaltation

Readings: Isa 1:10, 16-20; Matt 23:1-12

Scripture:
"The greatest among you must be your servant.
Whoever exalts himself will be humbled;
but whoever humbles himself will be exalted."
(Matt 23:11-12)

Reflection: Humility is one of those foundational virtues. This good habit enables us to live in the truth of things, to embrace reality for what it is, to accept our gifts and limitations as God sees them. Exaltation, by contrast, is a dangerous disposition, for it tends to lead to excessive pride and to a false sense of well-being. That being said, all those who serve in love and are humble will be raised up (exalted) by God in due time.

Saint Francis of Assisi exemplifies humility. He was keenly aware of God's mercy in his life. Everything was gift. Saint Francis served others by being an instrument of God's peace and joy. Today he is exalted as one of the most influential ambassadors of God's love and compassion. Francis's sins, though like scarlet, became white as snow through Jesus' cross; Francis's virtues, humility, joy, and peace, have become the paradigm of discipleship.

Jesus' parable of the Pharisee and the publican who came to the temple to pray is a fitting example of exaltation (Luke 18:9-14). The Pharisee did all the right things—he prayed, tithed, fasted. He even claimed not to be like the rest of humanity with its sins of greed, lust, and indulgence. The end of the parable is telling: the sinful publican, who admitted his faults, went home justified, not the self-exalting Pharisee.

Greatness is manifest in service; holiness, in humility. Lent calls us to serve and be humble. Come Easter, there might be some cause for exaltation.

Meditation: Who are the people in your life who demonstrate authentic humility? What is it about them that is so attractive? Is there a distinction between false and genuine exaltation?

Prayer: Gracious God, make us meek and humble of heart. Instill in us the joy of service; instill in us a love for lower places. Continue to send into our lives people like St. Francis who show us the way of true discipleship. We ask this in Jesus' name. Amen.

Q & A

Readings: Jer 18:18-20; Matt 20:17-28

Scripture:
Heed me, O LORD,
   and listen to what my adversaries say.
Must good be repaid with evil
   that they should dig a pit to take my life? (Jer 18:19-20a)

Reflection: As we ponder God's word, be it the Old or New Testament, many questions arise. In today's reading there are three: Jeremiah asks God why goodness must be repaid with malice; Jesus asks the mother of James and John what she wants for them; and Jesus confronts James and John with the question of whether or not they can share in the Lord's Supper by drinking from the same chalice he drinks from.
   And what are the answers?
   The only answer to why malice follows a good deed can be the misuse of freedom. Sin, it is, that brings about evil in the human heart. Be it jealousy or envy, anger or greed, pride or lust, choices are made that injure, even destroy, relationships. Jesus, like Jeremiah, did good by preaching, teaching, and healing. Yet we know that he was repaid with evil by being condemned to death, scourged, and crucified. However we interpret the behavior of the chief priests and scribes, sin is at the root of their actions.

Mothers have wishes for their children: good health, happiness, a long life. The mother of the sons of Zebedee wanted more: that her sons have a prominent place in the kingdom, prominent as in sitting right next to Jesus. She went for the works. We might ponder during this holy season what we want from God: a good conscience, freedom from self-regard, more courage, a better sense of humor. Or do we want a special place in the kingdom?

The third question is a challenging one: Can James and John, can you and I, participate in the suffering of Jesus, be it physical, psychological, or spiritual? Drinking from this chalice is essential in the life of discipleship. The paschal mystery is one of full participation. By sharing in the Lord's life and suffering, we can then share in his resurrection and glory.

Meditation: What are your Lenten questions? What do you want? Are you willing to share in the Lord's pain? Does doing good lead to evil consequences?

Prayer: Jesus, our Lord and Savior, we long to share in the mystery of your life. Give us the wisdom to ask the right questions; give us the courage to live the answers. May we follow James and John in their life of dedicated discipleship.

Rich Man, Poor Man

Readings: Jer 17:5-10; Luke 16:19-31

Scripture:
Jesus said to the Pharisees:
   "There was a rich man who dressed in purple garments
      and fine linen
   and dined sumptuously each day.
And lying at his door was a poor man named Lazarus
   . . ." (Luke 16:19-20a)

Reflection: Prophetic statements are disturbing. Listen to what Basil the Great wrote: "The money in your vaults belongs to the destitute. You do injustice to every man you could help but did not." It's difficult to sleep after hearing this, especially if one believes it to be true.

The rich man in today's parable had wealth, fine clothing, and good food. He also had a stingy disposition. He would not share even crumbs from the table with a poor beggar. We know the rest of the story and it does not have a happy ending.

The question of possession is troubling. One has the responsibility of providing for the future, both for oneself and one's family. This will entail some type of financial planning to fulfill that obligation. But the issue will arise: When is enough, enough? And yet another imperative: we have a duty to help those less fortunate and especially those in dire need. The tension here demands prayerful discernment and bold action.

The rich man was not totally self-absorbed. He did have concern for his brothers and pleaded that they might be warned about their impending doom. Apparently, even someone coming back from the dead would not startle them into change. The parable forces us to ask what it would take in our lives to become authentic stewards of God's gifts.

Behind the story line is the issue of trust, the type of trust that Jeremiah speaks about. If we trust in God, we can "afford" to be generous, even extravagant, with our possessions. God will provide even in the year of drought if we have faith. The rich man lacked more than generosity. He lacked a radical trust in a generous God.

Meditation: What is your relationship with the poor? List the names of "poor people" you have helped and who have helped you. When is enough, enough?

Prayer: Generous God, grant us the grace of your liberality. Help us to be extravagant in reaching out to those in need. You have given us so much. May our gratitude find expression in lives of generosity.

The Joseph/Jesus Stories

Readings: Gen 37:3-4, 12-13a, 17b-28a; Matt 21:33-43, 45-46

Scripture:
Israel loved Joseph best of all his sons,
    for he was the child of his old age;
    and he had made him a long tunic.
When his brothers saw that their father loved him best of
        all his sons,
    they hated him so much that they would not even greet
        him. (Gen 37:3-4)

Reflection: Many of us have seen the popular musical *Joseph and the Amazing Technicolor Dreamcoat*. This fast-moving production is filled with music and color, humor and satire. But beneath it all is a story, a powerful story of Joseph who was sold into slavery by his own brothers and would eventually be their salvation.

It is also a story of a father's love, but a love slightly misguided. The basic course of "Parenting 101" begins with a principle that a parent should not show favoritism, such as giving special gifts to one child and not to the others. Such behavior becomes the source of envy that would grow into anger, hatred, and even death. The Genesis story is a case in point.

In some subconscious fashion, the chief priests and elders in today's gospel sensed that Jesus was unique and special, indeed, loved in a special way by the Father. Jesus wore no dreamcoat, but he wore the gifts of compassion, love, and forgiveness. These qualities characterized his whole life. It was too much for the elders and the chief priests. This Jesus was beginning to win over the people and thereby threaten the established leadership. Like Joseph, he must be done away with. While Joseph escaped death, Jesus did not. But the Lord's death led to our salvation.

We might take the communion antiphon for our Lenten reflection today: "God loved us, and sent his Son / as expiation for our sins" (1 John 4:10).

Meditation: Why is parental favoritism so dangerous? In what ways has God gifted you? What meaning does the Joseph story have for you?

Prayer: Jesus, you are the beloved of the Father. Like Joseph, you faced hostility and hatred that would eventually lead to your death. Strengthen us on our journey so that we too might be obedient and strong in doing the Father's will. Be our salvation, Lord Jesus.

The God Question

Readings: Mic 7:14-15, 18-20; Luke 15:1-3, 11-32

Scripture:
Who is there like you, the God who removes guilt
  and pardons sin for the remnant of his inheritance;
Who does not persist in anger forever,
  but delights rather in clemency . . . (Mic 7:18)

Reflection: The God question never goes away. Who is this God that various world religions claim is the one, true deity? Different answers are given by the followers of Judaism, Buddhism, Hinduism, Islam, and Christianity. Turning to their sacred texts and traditions, they each offer their "theology," their attempt to describe and articulate their understanding of their faith.

In today's passage from Micah, we are told a number of things about the mystery of God: God shepherds his people, God shows wonderful signs, God removes guilt and pardons sins, God does not persist in anger, God delights in clemency and has compassion, God casts sin into the depths of the sea, and God is faithful.

Then in Luke's gospel, we are given a picture of God arising out of a parable. God is like the father of a Prodigal Son who never gives up on his children. More, this father offers forgiveness and reconciliation and goes far beyond this in throwing a party and feast for a wayward son. Jesus' Father is a God of extravagant mercy, a Father who longs for the return of those who are lost.

In her brilliant work *Creative Prayer*, Brigid E. Herman (1876–1923) warns the reader of the danger of having "a crude and childish conception of God." For an authentic spiritual life, one must, through grace and study, seek a mature concept of God, one that is discovered through Scripture, the writings of the saints, and personal experience. Only when our faith is grounded in a solid theology will our Lenten journey yield peace and joy.

Meditation: How has your understanding of God changed over the last five, ten years? What are the sources that deepen your knowledge and love of God? What does the parable of the Prodigal Son tell you about God's nature?

Prayer: Merciful and loving God, grant us wisdom to understand more deeply who you are. Grant us the grace of love to worship and adore you in your very essence. Our intellects are so limited; our affection so shallow. Send your Spirit of knowledge and understanding into our lives.

Remarkable Sights

Readings: Exod 3:1-8a, 13-15; 1 Cor 10:1-6, 10-12; Luke 13:1-9

Scripture:
There [Mt. Horeb] an angel of the LORD appeared to Moses
   in fire
   flaming out of a bush.
As he looked on, he was surprised to see that the bush,
   though on fire, was not consumed. (Exod 3:2)

Reflection: In the book of Exodus we hear Moses exclaim, "I must go over to look at this remarkable sight, and see why the bush is not burned" (Exod 3:3). In writing to the Corinthians Paul makes mention of their ancestors living under a cloud and passing through the sea—remarkable sights, indeed. Then Jesus, in Luke's gospel, tells of yet another remarkable sight: the fruitless fig tree and its impending doom.

During this Lenten season we are invited to have a sense of wonder and amazement at what God is doing in history, in our lives. First of all, we all dwell on sacred ground, God's creation. We do well to remove our sandals and reverence all that God has made, be it bushes, birds, babies, baboons. For those with eyes to see and ears to hear, creation reveals to us aspects of God's mystery. Moses encountered God as fire, a fire that transformed and did not consume. That same fire burns within us, a transforming, nonconsuming blaze. That fire is the gift of the Holy Spirit.

Like St. Paul, we do not want to be unaware of how God works in salvation history. Just as God guided the Israelites on their long journey to faith and freedom, the Lord guides us under the cloud of his love through the sea of his mercy. This God now gives us, in Jesus, the spiritual food and drink of the Eucharist. What a remarkable sight to see the diversity of so many nationalities coming together around the unity of the person of Christ. By living a eucharistic life, a life of love, compassion, and forgiveness, we are doing what is pleasing to God.

A constant challenge is to read the signs of the times, be those signs minor or major, ordinary or remarkable. Of course, the most remarkable sign of all time is God's abiding love for us in Jesus through the Holy Spirit. Indeed, the kingdom of God is at hand.

Meditation: What are the remarkable sights you have seen during these first weeks of Lent? What is the difference between a transforming and a consuming fire? How can repentance become a way of life?

Prayer: Lord God, both Moses and St. Paul have taught us much about your presence and love. Make us attentive to the power of Scripture; help us to shape our thoughts and values in accordance with your word. Send the fire of your Spirit into our lives so that we may follow your call and share your life.

The Good/Evil Paradox

Readings: 2 Kgs 5:1-15ab; Luke 4:24-30

Scripture:
Now the Arameans had captured in a raid on the land of
   Israel
   a little girl, who became the servant of Naaman's wife.
      (2 Kgs 5:2)

Reflection: That good can come out of evil is a strange fact. When Joseph was sold into slavery by his brothers, a deed most heinous, the story eventually had a happy ending. When Jesus was condemned and crucified, betrayed by a disciple, redemption was won through the mystery of the cross. When a little girl was taken from her family in a raid, a horrendous crime, that youth proved to be an instrument of healing.

So much evil; so much good. The prophets, be they Elisha or Elijah or Jesus himself, lived in a world filled with evil and goodness. The prophetic task was one of truth, helping people to discern light from darkness, life from death, love from hatred. In criticizing what was not of God and in offering hope through new possibilities, the prophets proved to be spiritual guides. But we know their fate. Because people preferred darkness to light, the prophets were driven out of town, often killed. Jesus, in his own hometown of Nazareth, experienced rejection and hostility.

Back to Naaman, the army commander. He was highly respected and esteemed by his master. He was also arrogant and condescending to outside help in dealing with his illness of leprosy. Running out of options, Naaman took the plunge into the Jordan River seven times, and healing filled both his body and his soul. We might even say that the "evil" of leprosy led to the "goodness" of faith in the God of Israel.

Meditation: Do you have any experiences of evil resulting in goodness? As a disciple of Jesus, in what way are you called to be a prophet, a bearer of truth?

Prayer: Lord Jesus, draw us to the Jordan River so that we might be cleansed of the leprosy of our sins. During this Lenten season, help us to see the evil we do; help us to do the good you command. May we, by our lives, be a prophetic sign of your love and mercy.

God's Forgiving Heart

Readings: Dan 3:25, 34-43; Matt 18:21-35

Scripture:
"His master summoned him and said to him, 'You wicked
    servant!
I forgave you your entire debt because you begged me to.
Should you not have had pity on your fellow servant,
    as I had pity on you?'" (Matt 18:32-33)

Reflection: The verse before the gospel is extremely consoling: "Even now, says the LORD, / return to me with your whole heart; / for I am gracious and merciful." Such is our God: "gracious and merciful, slow to anger" and rich in kindness. Made in the image and likeness of this God, we are to conform our lives according to the nature of our Maker.

Easier said than done. The doing of forgiveness calls for grace and a heart of pity and compassion. In the face of hurt and injury, we tend to hold grudges and resentment, bitterness and blatant hostility. Two responses are common: revenge or avoidance. God will have none of this. We are to forgive as we are forgiven; we are to extend compassion as we have received that gift from God.

In her book *The How of Happiness: A New Approach to Getting the Life You Want*, Sonja Lyubomirsky tells the story of Amy Biehl, a doctoral student who was killed by four young men in South Africa. Amy's parents, two years later, traveled to South Africa to console the killers' families. Here is big-time forgiveness; here is the gospel lived in spades.

The question of frequency—how often must we forgive?—is raised by Peter. Our standard is God's standard: forgiveness has no limit. For God forgiveness is yet another face of love: love expressed in the face of sin. Lent is a season of forgiveness and reconciliation, received and given.

Meditation: What is the difference between reconciliation and forgiveness? How often have you been forgiven? How often have you forgiven others?

Prayer: God of love and mercy, instill in us your grace of compassion and pity. Help us emulate you in the art of forgiveness. Without your grace, we will fail. With your help, we will extend your peace and, yes, joy to others.

A Wise and Intelligent People

Readings: Deut 4:1, 5-9; Matt 5:17-19

Scripture:
Moses spoke to the people and said: . . .
"Observe them [God's statutes and decrees] carefully,
   for thus will you give evidence
   of your wisdom and intelligence to the nations,
   who will hear of all these statutes and say,
   'This great nation is truly a wise and intelligent
     people.'" (Deut 4:6)

Reflection: Both Moses and Jesus instructed the people of their day to follow the law and commandments of God. It was precisely in being obedient to what God asked and demanded that one's intelligence and wisdom was made manifest. Stupidity and foolishness lay in disobedience, in drifting far from the paths of God's will.

Moses warned his people not to forget the ways of the Lord. Rather, they were not only to embrace God's law but they were to teach their children what God required of them. By so doing they would be known as a great nation in that they knew and lived the truth.

Jesus was not one to abolish the teachings of the prophet; nor did he abolish the law. Rather, he fulfilled what the prophets and the law taught. He was the new Moses and the greatest of all the prophets. Jesus' focus was always on the kingdom of God, that way of life in which his Father reigned and governed all the movements of one's life. The bottom line of the law and the prophets was love, a love given so that it might be passed on. By living the law of love one fulfilled God's will.

Education is one dimension of wisdom and intelligence. Diplomas on the wall do manifest some level of erudition. But a deeper wisdom and a more profound sign of intelligence is that of knowing and living the commandment of love. Those who embrace this way of life are great in God's kingdom.

Meditation: Who are the wise and intelligent people in your life? What are their characteristics? Who is greatest in God's kingdom?

Prayer: Lord Jesus, teach us to understand and live your commandment of love. We yearn to be a truly wise and intelligent people, a nation that is compassionate and caring. It is in obedience to your Father's will that we fulfill all that the law dictates and all that the prophets taught. Send us your Spirit so that we might be faithful to our vocation of love.

Walking in God's Ways

Readings: Jer 7:23-28; Luke 11:14-23

Scripture:
Thus says the Lord:
　This is what I command my people:
　　Listen to my voice;
　　then I will be your God and you shall be my people.
Walk in all the ways that I command you,
　so that you may prosper. (Jer 7:23)

Reflection: Our responsorial refrain—"If today you hear his voice, harden not your hearts" (Ps 95:8)—sets the tone for today's liturgy. God speaks to us through Scripture, in the cry of the poor, in the inner movements of our heart, through the richness of our sacramental life. The challenge is listening, a most difficult art for us humans. So many voices seek our attention and elicit our commitment. To whom or to what do we listen?

But listening (and responding) depends upon the texture of our hearts. We hear in the Jeremiah passage that the people "walked in the hardness of their evil hearts." We can sense that hardness in the gospel as Jesus is tested by members of the crowd for driving out a demon from a mute man. Rather than listening and seeing the compassion of God made manifest in Jesus, they question this great act of kindness and healing. Hardness of heart does such things.

It is in Ezekiel the prophet that we find much hope. In chapter 36, verses 24-28, we are told that God will give us a new heart and a new spirit. Perhaps another way of looking at conversion is through the lens of a heart transplant. When we put on the mind and heart of Christ, we see, feel, and act in a different fashion. Then, and only then, will we walk in the ways of the Lord.

Meditation: Why is listening such a difficult task? What are some signs that our hearts are hard, signs that our hearts are of a graced texture?

Prayer: Loving God, may we walk in your ways. Give us hearts of flesh so that we may follow in the way of your Son Jesus. Too long have we wandered from your mercy; too long have we failed to hear and obey your voice. Grant us the gift of the Holy Spirit.

God's Kingdom: Far or Near?

Readings: Hos 14:2-10; Mark 12:28-34

Scripture:
And when Jesus saw that he [one of the scribes] answered
    with understanding,
  he said to him,
  "You are not far from the Kingdom of God."
    (Mark 12:34a)

Reflection: There is a significant distance between wise understanding and the doing of truth. The scribe in today's gospel grasped the meaning of God's commandments. By so doing, he was not far from God's reign. But more was needed to actually participate in God's kingdom: loving God and one's neighbor totally.

In the book of the prophet Hosea we are made aware of human guilt and God's forgiveness and love. At the end of today's passage we read, "Let him who is wise understand these things; / let him who is prudent know them. / Straight are the paths of the LORD, / in them the just walk, / but sinners stumble in them" (Hos 14:10). Again we see the difference between understanding and doing, knowledge and action, appreciation and achievement. Prophets have not only the task of enlightening us to see clearly but also the challenge to doing the truth in love. In fulfilling this vocation, they participate in God's kingdom, even though it often endangers their physical well-being.

Saint Thomas Aquinas (1225–74), a Doctor of the Church, spoke eloquently of the virtue of prudence, that perfected ability in life to make right decisions. Three things are necessary in the life of prudent persons: deliberation, judgment, and action. It is by means of this virtue that we draw near to the kingdom of God. Through deliberation, we come to understand God's commandments; through judgment, we decide to act in accord with God's plan; through action, we do God's will with courage and love. Only through prudence can we also be just, courageous, and temperate, all qualities of God's kingdom.

Meditation: What is the difference for you between understanding and action? Who are the prudent people in your life? Why is prudence the mother virtue of the other moral virtues: justice, fortitude, and temperance?

Prayer: Lord Jesus, give us the grace to participate in your kingdom by understanding and living your commandment of love. Too easily we live lives of self-indulgence. Help us to transcend our own needs and be for others as you were for others through your life of self-giving and obedience. Come, Lord Jesus, come.

A Saved Wretch

Readings: Hos 6:1-6; Luke 18:9-14

Scripture:
"But the tax collector stood off at a distance
   and would not even raise his eyes to heaven
   but beat his breast and prayed,
   'O God, be merciful to me a sinner.'" (Luke 18:13)

Reflection: Some years ago there was an article lamenting the fact that people were reluctant to include the word "wretch" in the first verse of the hymn "Amazing Grace." Few of us appreciate being labeled a wretch, a miserable person, one who is despised and held in contempt. The school of positive psychology will have none of this. The "I'm OK, you're OK" culture demands that we change the lyrics of "Amazing Grace" or any other song that puts us in a bad light.

   Yet the old tax collector in Jesus' parable "beat his breast" and knew, deep down, that he was a sinner. Whether he was "greedy, dishonest, adulterous" we do not know. What we do know is that he knew himself a sinner and sought God's mercy. In his humble prayer, he went home justified by God's merciful grace.

   A father was teaching his third-grade daughter her prayers. When they came to the Hail Mary, the little girl questioned her dad. "Daddy, why do I have to tell Mary that I am a sinner and that she must pray for me now and at the hour of my death? I don't think I'm going to die very soon and I don't think I am a big sinner."

In a hymnal on my bookshelf, there is an optional text for the first line of "Amazing Grace." Instead of singing "Amazing grace! / How sweet the sound / That saved a wretch like me!" we are offered an alternative: "Amazing grace! How sweet the sound / That saved and set me free!" The tax collector would probably prefer the original text.

Meditation: Why is it so difficult (if not downright disgusting) to see ourselves as sinners? How do you react to the second half of the Hail Mary?

Prayer: Lord Jesus, help us to fathom the depth of your parables. Draw us into your stories so that we might understand what qualities of the Pharisee and of the tax collector reside in our souls. May we come to the truth of things and embrace the grace of humility. We long to be justified by your love and mercy.

The Ministry of Reconciliation

Readings: Josh 5:9a, 10-12; 2 Cor 5:17-21; Luke 15:1-3, 11-32

Scripture:
So we are ambassadors for Christ,
    as if God were appealing through us.
We implore you on behalf of Christ,
    be reconciled to God. (2 Cor 5:20)

Reflection: In his *Principles of Christian Theology*, the Anglican scholar John Macquarrie speaks of reconciliation as the healing of the disorders of existence, the redressing of imbalances, and the bridging over of alienations.

Sin causes disorder. Saint Paul tells us, in his letter to the Romans, that he is unable to do what he wants to do and does things that he doesn't want to do. Paul experienced disorder. And this stressful situation is *after* his conversion. That means that for St. Paul and all of us, reconciliation and conversion are lifelong processes. In all of our lives there will always be some disorders, be they sensual, psychological, intellectual, or spiritual. We stand in need of the presence of Christ to attain some order and harmony on this perilous journey.

Sin causes imbalances. The old philosophical principle holds true: virtue stands in the middle. Yet we tend toward excess: too much food, too little food; too much work, too little work; too many possessions, too few essentials for humane living. It's hard to get it right! Even Jesus was attacked when he and his disciples ate and drank, and did not fast. Having the mind and heart of Christ helps us to keep proper balance on the journey.

Sin causes alienation. Both the Prodigal Son and his elder brother sinned and stood in need of reconciliation. The one wasted his father's inheritance; the other resented the father's gratuitous celebration and extravagant mercy. Reconciliation bridges over these family disputes and broken relationships.

During Lent we are called to be both reconciled to God and agents of reconciliation. As Christ's ambassadors, we say yes to the call to heal relationships, to deal with the disorders of existence (our own and others'), and to name and address the imbalances that are part of our experience. When we undertake this mission, Christ will always be the lead agent and we his coworkers. God does appeal through us in continuing the work of redemption.

Meditation: What is your understanding of reconciliation? Are you able to name the disorders of your existence, your imbalances, and your areas of alienation? How is Jesus' mission of redemption manifest in your life?

Prayer: God of mercy and forgiveness, give us the grace to foster the union and unity you desire. May we be your instruments of reconciliation, your ambassadors of good news. Just as you reconcile us to yourself in Jesus, may we participate in this ministry by sharing your healing with others.

Near Death

Readings: Isa 65:17-21; John 4:43-54

Scripture:
Now there was a royal official whose son was ill in
    Capernaum.
When he heard that Jesus had arrived in Galilee from
    Judea,
    he went to him and asked him to come down
    and heal his son, who was near death. (John 4:46b-47)

Reflection: When children die before their parents, we sense that something is terribly wrong. This is not the order of things, doubling grief and compounding the mystery of death. Any of us who have had a sibling who died before our parents know the agony of such a loss.

The royal official who came to Jesus must have heard about the miracle at Cana when Jesus turned water into wine. Perhaps, just perhaps, this prophet who had compassion at the wedding feast might extend that compassion to his son who was near death. So the official made his request: "Sir, come down before my child dies" (John 4:49). Jesus' heart was moved with pity. The son would live.

What happened at Capernaum in Galilee fulfilled the promise given through the prophet Isaiah: "No longer shall the sound of weeping be heard there, / or the sound of crying; / No longer shall there be in it / an infant who lives but a few days" (Isa 65:19b-20a). One can only imagine the rejoicing that went on in the household of the royal official as the fever left the youth. Forever, for the rest of his life, these words would echo in the heart of that official: "You may go; your son will live" (John 4:50a).

Jesus is the resurrection and the life. Those who believe come to experience that, whether we die young or old, we are the Lord's and the promise of eternal life will be fulfilled. It is faith that gives us confidence that both sin and death have been conquered through the paschal mystery.

Meditation: What is your reaction to news that someone is near death? How deep is your faith in the power of the resurrection, the power that it conquers even death itself?

Prayer: Lord Jesus, we trust in your compassion and love. Grant health to those who are ill; grant consolation to those who suffer the loss of a loved one. Be with us in our joys and sorrows. Give us the strength to embrace whatever comes, be it life or death.

Having No One

Readings: Ezek 47:1-9, 12; John 5:1-16

Scripture:
The sick man answered him [Jesus],
  "Sir, I have no one to put me into the pool
  when the water is stirred up;
  while I am on my way, someone else gets down there
    before me." (John 5:7)

Reflection: Do you have someone, someone who will be with you and for you on life's journey? The sick man in today's gospel had no one and therefore was helpless when the sacred waters stirred with new life. Then Jesus came, the servant of all, and cured him on the spot even though it was the Sabbath.

To crawl inside those words—"I have no one"—is to experience existential loneliness. In the first book of the Bible we are told that it is not good to be alone. We are social in nature and our physical, social, psychological, and spiritual well-being is dependent upon friends and community. One of the greatest mistakes in life is to travel alone.

Jesus ventured down to the pool of Bethesda and encountered people who were ill, lame, crippled, and blind. He went where the suffering was to bring healing and hope. As servant he was "for" others; as prophet and teacher he was "with" others, instructing them in the ways of the kingdom of God.

The good that Jesus did raised objections. After all, it was the Sabbath and such activity on this day was contrary to the law. Jesus' compassion transcended any legalism; Jesus' love was *the* law. Though only in the fourth week of Lent, we are beginning to see the price that Jesus will pay for this work of redemption. Persecution would follow but it would not prevent the Lord's mission from being accomplished.

Meditation: Who are the people in your life who travel with you so that you never have to say that you have no one? Whom do you assist on the journey so that they too never have to say that they have no one?

Prayer: Lord Jesus, we all desire to be well. Come and heal us of our loneliness and fears, of our pride and greed. At times we travel alone and have no one to comfort or challenge us. Be with us always; be for us always. We trust in you.

Intimacy: A Graced Threat

Readings: Isa 49:8-15; John 5:17-30

Scripture:
But Zion said, "The Lord has forsaken me;
  my Lord has forgotten me."
Can a mother forget her infant,
  be without tenderness for the child of her womb?
Even should she forget,
  I will never forget you. (Isa 49:14-15)

Reflection: The intimacy between a mother and the infant in her womb is indescribable. So too the intimacy between Jesus and his Father. There is a oneness here, within the mystery of the Trinity, that theologians have been pondering for centuries and of whose glory even the mystics have only a faint glimmer. But for that, the intimacy is there, causing wonder and amazement to the observant.

The mother/infant and Father/Son intimacy is an experience that stirs the human heart. One of the deepest hungers of the heart, if not *the* deepest, is this desire for union with God and unity with one another. In fact, redemption is about oneness. Jesus came so that we might, through love and God's mercy, come to know this happiness. The by-products of authentic intimacy and union are peace and joy.

But something has gone wrong. Sin separates and divides; sin causes alienation and hostility. Jesus faced that hostility when he was accused of making himself equal to the Father. Isaiah the prophet speaks about darkness and affliction and how God will bring about the day of salvation. All of this is a matter of life and death, of resurrection or condemnation.

In her novel *The Violent Bear It Away*, Flannery O'Connor describes a character who did everything in his power to avoid "this threatened intimacy of creation." All of us are "threatened" by the intimacy of creation, redemption, and sanctification. Let us pray that we embrace and not avoid it.

Meditation: What is your experience of intimacy? Why is union with God and unity with one another so difficult?

Prayer: Lord God, you call us to be one with you. Give us the grace to be grasped by your tender love and mercy. May we never fear your call to intimacy; may we never hesitate to share your love with one another.

A Stiff-Necked People

Readings: Exod 32:7-14; John 5:31-47

Scripture:
The LORD said to Moses,
  "I see how stiff-necked this people is.
Let me alone, then,
    that my wrath may blaze up against them to consume
      them.
Then I will make of you a great nation." (Exod 32:9-10)

Reflection: Our human anatomy often expresses our interior states, be it weak knees, hardness of heart, or a stiff neck. These expressions indicate a lack of courage, want of love or affection, and a stubbornness that makes rigid our way of life. Such dispositions alienate us from God, from others, and even ourselves. This alienation leads to the impression that God is angry and wrathful, contradicting our faith that God is absolute love and mercy.

We witness in the mission of John the Baptist ("a burning and shining lamp") and in the ministry of Jesus the divine plan of salvation. God sends into the world great prophets and teachers to proclaim the truth and to call people to conversion. Moses had his work to do as did John and Jesus. But, time and time again, obstacles arose: idolatry (molten calf), pride, jealousy, sloth, and the list goes on. Yet God remains faithful and, to this day, mentors and models are sent to draw us from darkness to light, from sin to grace.

In his novel *Eternity, My Beloved*, Jean Sulivan forcefully writes, "To believe you can change your ideas without a change of heart, and that you can achieve this change of heart without changing your life-style, is the illusion of many, an incurable illusion." Conversion is multidimensional. It involves a change of heart, a change of lifestyle, a change of thinking. Only through the grace of God and the support of others will we enter and stay in the process of conversion.

Meditation: What part of your anatomy speaks of the need for conversion? How has your thinking, feeling, and acting changed in the last five years? Who are the mentors and models that help you to follow in the ways of God?

Prayer: Lord Jesus, you call us to repentance. So often we are stiff-necked and ill-disposed to your divine pleasure. Send us the Spirit of courage so that we may face what needs changing and the grace of hope not to become discouraged. May this season of Lent be a time of renewal for all of us.

Whence and Whither

Readings: Wis 2:1a, 12-22; John 7:1-2, 10, 25-30

Scripture:
Could the authorities have realized that he is the Christ?
But we know where he is from.
When the Christ comes, no one will know where he is
    from. (John 7:26b-27)

Reflection: "Where are you from?" This question is often asked upon meeting someone new. A person's origin, his or her geography, is an important factor in identity. So when the origin of Jesus was raised, a serious issue was put on the table.

Our Christology tells us that Jesus was begotten by the Father from all eternity. The Son of God was with the Father and the Spirit from all eternity. Here we plunge into the great mystery of the Trinity, our one God in three persons. When Jesus was conceived and born of Mary, we were given a second great mystery: the incarnation. Upon these two mysteries, the Trinity and the incarnation, our faith is grounded.

So where was Jesus from and where was he bound? Yes, he came from Nazareth in Galilee; yes, he came from the Father; yes, he still comes to us in word and sacrament. And his destiny? After his mission on earth was completed, Jesus would return to the Father in glory. The mysteries of the resurrection and ascension give us the answer to the "whither" as does his birth answer the question of the "whence."

As we reflect upon the origin and destiny of Jesus, we are invited to ponder the source of our being and the goal of our life. Like Jesus, we came from God; like Jesus, we are destined toward eternal life. Did the authorities in Jesus' time realize this about themselves? If so, they would not be so bold and arrogant in their exercise of power.

Meditation: How has your place of origin shaped your life? How have you grown in your understanding of the Trinity and incarnation over the years?

Prayer: Jesus, help us to deepen our knowledge and love of you and the Father. Send your Spirit of wisdom and understanding upon us. May we follow in the way you traveled, reaching out to the needy, caring for the ill, and sharing our life with the downtrodden. Then, after our discipleship, may we and our sisters and brothers share eternity with you.

What Is He Doing?

Readings: Jer 11:18-20; John 7:40-53

Scripture:
Nicodemus, one of their members who had come to him
      [Jesus] earlier, said to them [the crowd],
  "Does our law condemn a man before it first hears him
  and finds out what he is doing?" (John 7:50-51)

Reflection: Jesus often warns his disciples and the crowds not to judge or condemn. Rather, we are to have understanding and compassion in evaluating what we and others do. And what is it that Jesus does? Heals, teaches, preaches, and saves! That is quite a resume that defies condemnation.

But then Jesus does heal on the Sabbath; Jesus teaches by way of parables that convict his listeners; Jesus preaches love of everyone, even one's enemies; and, Jesus saves sinners. This is too much for the righteous; this is too much for those who have other messages than that of love, forgiveness, and compassion. So the plotting begins to get rid of this so-called prophet from Galilee, a land supposedly devoid of the prophetic ministry.

In the face of all this, Nicodemus brings a call to justice. No judgment without a hearing; no condemnation without evidence. But all this to no avail. Jesus, like Jeremiah, is "a trusting lamb led to slaughter" (Jer 11:19a), a tree cut down in its prime. Prophets do not fare well in history.

In her spiritual reflections, *The Reed of God*, Caryll Houselander observes that our judgments more often arise from our own fears, needs, and limitations, seldom from "an objective contemplation." If that is the case, we should all refrain from judging our brothers and sisters, much less the activities of God.

Meditation: What is the history of your judging, your judgment of self and others? Do you agree with Caryll Houselander that most judgments arise out of our limitations, fears, and needs?

Prayer: Lord Jesus, you are *the* prophet, who brings truth to our dark world. Not only do you teach us the Father's will, you do it. Make us instruments of the kingdom; make us instruments of your peace and joy. Forgive us our judgments and grant us compassion.

Something New!

Readings: Isa 43:16-21; Phil 3:8-14; John 8:1-11

Scripture:
Remember not the events of the past,
　the things of long ago consider not;
see, I am doing something new!
　Now it springs forth, do you not perceive it?
　　(Isa 43:18-19a)

Reflection: The woman in the gospel perceived it, this something new. It was the compassion of God revealed in Jesus. Saint Paul perceived it, this something new. In experiencing the mystery of Christ, he considered everything, by comparison, to be rubbish. All the great saints perceived it, this something new. It was the experience of God's grace that came to them unmerited, totally gratuitous.

We should include in this listing the psalmist who sings out in our responsorial refrain, "The Lord has done great things for us; we are filled with joy" (Ps 126:3). At the center of those great things is liberation, being freed from our captivity to sin and death. The woman caught in adultery was liberated when Jesus told her that he did not condemn her. What joy must have raced through her heart. What gratitude must have filled her being in not only being freed from the law's command that she be stoned but also from the guilt and shame that are the consequences of sin. Probably, for the rest of her life, she turned every night to Psalm 126 and lifted her voice in song.

Saint Paul experienced that great liberation, that something new that set him free. After his conversion experience, he desired but one thing: to share in the suffering of Christ so as to share also in his glory. His life was consumed by the ministry of evangelization. By spreading the good news of our freedom in Christ, he would offer the possibility of peace and joy to the people of his own day and to us through his epistles. With single-mindedness Paul proclaims, "Just one thing: forgetting what lies behind but straining forward to what lies ahead, I continue my pursuit toward the goal, the prize of God's upward calling, in Christ Jesus" (Phil 3:13b-14).

During Lent we continue to reflect on the goal that St. Paul pursued, eternal life. Because of the mystery of Jesus' paschal mystery, we know that this goal is attainable in grace. Thus we live as a people freed, no longer enslaved to guilt and shame.

Meditation: What are the "new things" that you have experienced during this season of Lent? How has God liberated you from sin?

Prayer: Loving and merciful God, we give you thanks for your liberating grace, for making all things new in our life. We desire to sing of your goodness, to praise you for the wonders of your love. Be with us this day so that we may perceive the newness of life.

Light from Light

Readings: Dan 13:1-9, 15-17, 19-30, 33-62; John 8:12-20

Scripture:
Jesus spoke to them again, saying,
  "I am the light of the world.
Whoever follows me will not walk in darkness,
  but will have the light of life." (John 8:12)

Reflection: There are indeed greater and lesser lights. Just ask the sun; just ask the moon. But regardless of the intensity, light enables us to see and sometimes even to know, to know the face of a friend, to know the glorious colors of an autumn maple, to know who we are and where we are going.

Jesus is the *great* light. He is the presence and manifestation of God in our dark world. By being invited into his life, we become the agents of light and life and, oh yes, of love too. We participate in the great struggle that confronts evil. As George Eliot states in one of her novels, "we are part of the divine power against evil—widening the skirts of light and making the struggle with darkness narrower."

Ours is a dark world. History, page after page, reports the evils of nations as we read about human slaughter, the devastation of the earth, and exploitation of peoples. It is not a pretty picture. Jesus plunged into our history bearing the divine light and shining radiantly in the darkness. And even though his death appears as a defeat, we believe in the resurrection and that Jesus is truly the light of life.

Emily Dickinson wrote about that certain slant of light that we see in a late winter afternoon. Christians speak about that certain slant of light that broke into history in the mystery of the incarnation. No matter how dark the world may appear, no one and nothing will conquer that magical light of grace.

Meditation: Is the sun a symbol of grace for you? What role does light play in your spiritual life? What do you do to scatter the darkness of sin?

Prayer: Lord Jesus, you are our light and our life. So often we dwell in darkness and sin, in doubt and despair. Help us to see the work of your hand; help us to embrace the call to be light to others. May we widen "the skirts of light" by being your disciples. Come, Lord Jesus, come.

A Just and Upright Man

Readings: 2 Sam 7:4-5a, 12-14a, 16; Rom 4:13, 16-18, 22; Matt 1:16, 18-21, 24a

Scripture:
Jacob was the father of Joseph, the husband of Mary.
Of her was born Jesus who is called the Christ. (Matt 1:16)

Reflection: Jesus, Mary, Joseph! Son, mother, husband! Though some satirists claim that family life is overrated, we all know how important parents are to children, children to parents. Families are not only the fundamental social unit of any society but families also shape destinies. They can neither be overrated nor overappreciated.

We know very little about the Holy Family. But the things we do know are sufficient to give us insight into God's great plan of salvation: Jesus, son of God and son of Mary; Mary, full of grace and obedient to God's will; Joseph, just and righteous, doing what the angel bid him to do. Here are three individuals who were obedient to the Father's will, regardless of the huge price. What a model the Holy Family is for all of us.

To honor one member of the family is to honor them all. Today the universal church holds up St. Joseph as someone to emulate. As husband, stepfather, and breadwinner, Joseph was faithful to what God asked of him. His justice was an expression of obedience; his justice brought him peace and righteousness.

It is unfortunate that the only time some people turn to St. Joseph is when they are attempting to sell their homes. Were we to put a statue of St. Joseph in our kitchen (rather than buried in the backyard), we would be daily reminded of what the Christian life is all about: loving attention to God's presence. Such was the life of St. Joseph here on earth; such is the life of St. Joseph in heaven.

Meditation: In what way can St. Joseph be of assistance in living out our family life? In what way has your family shaped your destiny?

Prayer: Saint Joseph, pray for us. We live in times that are not family friendly. So many of our homes are broken; so many relationships are strained; so much abandonment is experienced. Help us to be attentive to God's loving presence so that we might hear and do the Father's will as you and Mary did.

March 20: Wednesday of the Fifth Week of Lent

Idolatry: An Ancient Sin?

Readings: Dan 3:14-20, 91-92, 95; John 8:31-42

Scripture:
King Nebuchadnezzar said:
  "Is it true, Shadrach, Meshach, and Abednego,
  that you will not serve my god,
  or worship the golden statue that I set up?" (Dan 3:14)

Reflection: In our first reading today, we hear about King Nebuchadnezzar, who serves his own god and worships a golden statue. Idolatry might appear to be a sin of ancient days but, sad to say, it is still alive and thriving in our own times. In our contemporary culture, many are willing to kneel before the molten calf of power or prestige, pleasure or possessions. In his novel *Midnight's Children*, Salman Rushdie speaks of another faith in India—namely, "Businessism." Even though we claim to be an "enlightened" people, we need but scratch the surface and idols can be found.

But then there are always individuals who remain faithful, regardless of the cost. We witness the courage of Shadrach, Meshach, and Abednego. We witness the courage of a St. Thomas More or St. Joan of Arc. We witness the fidelity of Blessed Mother Teresa of Calcutta or Blessed John Henry Newman. Through God's grace, all of these individuals kept their focus and believed in the one, true God.

And then there is Abraham, the father of faith. In the gospel, we hear about those who claim to be descendants of Abraham and yet they do not do the works of Abraham. Jesus rebukes them for that and forcefully reminds them that sin is slavery. Unless they do the will of God, they are not free.

It is paradoxical (and sad) that the popular *American Idol* program claims to be reality television. Our faith tells us that God is *the* reality, the fullness of truth, goodness, and beauty. To worship or serve anyone or anything else is a dead-end street.

Meditation: What are some of the idols that you have seen on your journey of life? Does everyone kneel and worship someone or something, be it their own ego, money, power, or the living and true God?

Prayer: Lord God, your faithful servants Shadrach, Meshach, and Abednego were willing to die rather than worship a golden statue. You gave them both the gift of faith and the gift of courage. Send those blessings into our hearts, for we are tempted in many ways. May your Spirit keep us faithful to you and your will.

Creation, Covenant, Community

Readings: Gen 17:3-9; John 8:51-59

Scripture:
God also said to Abraham:
   "On your part, you and your descendants after you
   must keep my covenant throughout the ages."
      (Gen 17:9)

Reflection: In his *Treatise on the Love of God*, St. Francis de Sales, a Doctor of the Church, discourses at length on doing the will of God. He is very clear in emphasizing that a significant part of God's will is adhering diligently to three things: the commandments, the counsels, and divine inspirations. Just as Abraham was instructed by God to keep the covenant, so we too are to keep the divine directives that lead to life.

In the gospel, Jesus asserts that people who keep his word will not taste death (John 8:52b). Though this was misunderstood by his hearers, we know that eternal life is promised to those who are faithful to Jesus' way of life. Discipleship involves a life of forgiving, loving, and being compassionate. Discipleship means listening and doing what God asks of us.

God's commandments are binding on everyone. Through obedience to the Decalogue, we protect and promote our relationship with God and with our neighbor. The counsels, such as sell everything and give it to the poor, apply to certain individuals in particular situations. Many parents could not follow this counsel and still support their children. Inspirations, through ongoing nudges, whispers, proddings, drawings that are the action of the Holy Spirit, are to be seriously discerned and followed. Every day these inner stirrings happen; every day God works in the depth of our being.

In the mystery of creation, God brought forth the world in all its splendor. In the mystery of the covenant, God established a unique relationship with a people. We are people of a new covenant and we are faithful to that covenant to the extent that we hear and do God's will.

Meditation: In what ways does God "inspire" you? Are you attentive to the inner stirrings and proddings of grace? What is your understanding of "covenant"?

Prayer: Gracious God, just as you drew Abraham into your covenant relationship, draw us into the circle of your life and love. Grant us the gift of discernment so that we might be attuned to your slightest stirring within our hearts. Grant us the grace of courage to respond fully and promptly to whatever you ask.

The Death Penalty Lives

Readings: Jer 20:10-13; John 10:31-42

Scripture:
The Jews picked up rocks to stone Jesus.
Jesus answered them, "I have shown you many good
   works from my Father.
For which of these are you trying to stone me?"
   (John 10:31-32)

Reflection: The death penalty has been around for a long time. Stephen, the first martyr, was stoned to death while Saul looked on. The woman caught in adultery was on the verge of the same cruel fate until Jesus intervened. Nations continue to execute criminals despite the fact that the poor and minorities are more often put to death than the rich and those more highly educated.

Jesus was on the list for execution. Though he was not stoned to death, he was crucified and the crime was supposed blasphemy. As we ponder the gospels, Jesus goes from town to town preaching, teaching, and healing. These are the good works that further the kingdom of his Father; these are the good works that we are to emulate in our own unique circumstances. It is all about bringing life, not death; promoting love, not hatred; fostering light, not darkness.

The first principle of Catholic social teaching is the value and dignity of human life. After that follow six more imperatives: call to family, community, and participation; rights and responsibilities; option for the poor and vulnerable; dignity of work and the rights of workers; solidarity; and care of God's creation. To the degree that we appropriate and live these principles, we too will be doing the good works assigned us by the Father.

In the movie *Dead Man Walking*, we witness the devastation wrought by heinous crimes. We also witness the horror of taking of human life. Again and again we are reminded that Jesus came to bring life, life to the full (John 10:10). Our work is to be agents of life and messengers of God's love and forgiveness.

Meditation: What is your stance regarding the death penalty? What good works are you doing this Lent to foster the expansion of God's kingdom?

Prayer: Lord Jesus, give us the compassion we need to understand the mind and heart of your Father. May your Spirit of life permeate our hearts. We desire to do the good works that you did, regardless of the cost. Guide us in your ways.

Believers and Nonbelievers

Readings: Ezek 37:21-28; John 11:45-56

Scripture:
Many of the Jews who had come to Mary
  and seen what Jesus had done began to believe in him.
But some of them went to the Pharisees
  and told them what Jesus had done. (John 11:45-46)

Reflection: The same experience can elicit totally different responses. For some individuals who experienced Jesus' preaching, teaching, and healing, their response was one of faith. For others, in the same synagogue, by the same seashore, at the same street corner, their response was one of nonacceptance.

Throughout history, Jesus has been embraced as Savior, Redeemer, and Friend. Throughout history, Jesus has been the object of scorn, ridicule, and betrayal. And all this is more than just human freedom being exercised in diverse ways. What we are dealing with is an event, the incarnation, that has forever changed history.

For those who saw and believed, significant demands followed. Now they must live a new life based on forgiveness, compassion, and love. They must love even their enemies, do good to the ungrateful, stop judging, and be compassionate to all. Faith called for a total commitment to discipleship and that involved a dying to oneself. Indeed, discipleship is costly, for it involves picking up one's cross daily and walking beside Jesus.

By not believing, people attempt to free themselves from the demands of the gospel. But it doesn't work. We are all made to God's image and likeness. Whoever we are and whatever our belief system, we can only be authentic and real to the extent that we embrace God's will.

The prophet Ezekiel delivered a foundational message to the people of his day and to us in the twenty-first century: "My dwelling shall be with them; / I will be their God, and they shall be my people" (Ezek 37:27).

Meditation: What are the things that Jesus has done for you on your faith journey? Why is faith such a costly affair?

Prayer: Loving God, open our minds and hearts to your divine revelation. As we approach Holy Week, may we see more deeply what Jesus continues to do for us. Deepen our faith in your abiding presence; deepen our hope in eternal life.

The Crucifix: A Symbol of God's Love

Readings: Isa 50:4-7; Phil 2:6-11; Luke 22:14–23:56

Scripture:
When they came to the place called the Skull,
   they crucified him and the criminals there,
   one on his right, the other on his left. (Luke 23:33)

Reflection: The sacramental principle informs us that God's grace, God's life-love-light, is mediated through signs and symbols. And is there any more powerful symbol than the crucifix? Before our gaze is the Redeemer of the world nailed to the tree of the cross. Here is the Son of God who was obedient unto death, death on the cross. Here is the mystery of our salvation in its raw beauty.

In the face of mystery, symbols are extremely important since the mind cannot comprehend the depth of what is taking place. That God's love would manifest itself so supremely on the cross confuses our human logic. It is by standing alongside Mary at the foot of the cross and experiencing her sorrow and anguish that we participate in the work of our salvation.

Other images on this Palm Sunday also reveal aspects of God's grace: the tearing of the temple veil as Jesus commended his spirit to the Father; the crowing of the cock that sent Peter into repentance; the blessing, breaking, and giving of the bread at the Passover meal; the spices and perfumed oil the women from Galilee used in Jesus' burial. As we hear the passion proclaimed, these images engage our imagination and hearts so that we might come to know the great price of our redemption.

Saint Teresa of Avila maintained that our ability to bear crosses, whether great or small, indicated the measure of our love. The cross that Jesus bore was great; the love that Jesus has for us is infinite.

Meditation: What are three Christian symbols that speak to you of God's grace? What role does the cross play in your life? Is the sacramental principle a deep part of your personal spirituality?

Prayer: Lord Jesus, Savior of the world and Redeemer of all, give us the grace to understand more deeply the mystery of the cross. Suffering intimidates us; pain elicits so many fears. We need your courage to participate in the work of redemption. As we stand at the foot of the cross with Mary, may our faith deepen, our hope be renewed, and our love increase a hundredfold.

March 25: Monday of Holy Week

"Ever Present Reality"

Readings: Isa 42:1-7; John 12:1-11

Scripture:
Thus says God, the LORD . . .
   I have grasped you by the hand;
I formed you, and set you
   as a covenant of the people,
   a light for the nations,
To open the eyes of the blind,
   to bring out prisoners from confinement,
   and from the dungeon, those who live in darkness.
    (Isa 42:5a, 6b-7)

Reflection: In his powerful work *On-Going Incarnation: Johann Adam Mohler and the Beginning of Modern Ecclesiology*, Fr. Michael Himes writes about the "ever present reality of being grasped, created, supported, and loved by God." This was the experience of Isaiah the prophet as he tells how God grasps us by the hand and never lets us go.

Jesus' relationship with the Father was one of intense intimacy. From that relationship his mission flowed: be a light to the nations, help the blind see, free prisoners, lead people out of darkness into the light. In doing the will of his Father, Jesus paid the price of martyrdom. In our liturgy today we witness his impending death as Judas is about to betray him and Mary anoints him in preparation for his burial.

For some reason Judas was not able to "grasp" that he was grasped and loved and supported by God. On the other hand, Mary, Martha, and Lazarus were able to believe in God's love revealed in Jesus. Here we have the great mystery of faith, experienced by some and not by others.

In this Holy Week we are invited to taste deeply that "ever present reality" of God's love and mercy. We might ask for the grace to understand the great grace of revelation. As Fr. Himes reminds us in his book on Mohler, the first revelation is creation but the special Christian revelation is the Trinity and the incarnation.

Meditation: Have you experienced the reality of being grasped by God? How do you help others to believe that they are created, supported, and loved by our gracious God?

Prayer: Lord Jesus, as we enter more deeply into Holy Week, may our faith in you and your work of redemption deepen. Through the mystery of your incarnation and the work of redemption, help us to experience God's ever abiding love. Grasp us by the hand and never let us go.

Troublemaker/Troubleshooter

Readings: Isa 49:1-6; John 13:21-33, 36-38

Scripture:
Jesus was deeply troubled and testified,
   "Amen, amen, I say to you, one of you will betray me."
The disciples looked at one another, at a loss as to whom
      he meant. (John 13:21-22)

Reflection: Troublemakers and troubleshooters are two very different types of personalities. The troublemaker causes agitation, anxiety, and often calamity. The troubleshooter is one who has the ability to locate and eliminate sources of disturbance.

Judas was a troublemaker. It is frightening to read that "Jesus was deeply troubled." He was troubled for a number of reasons: the betrayal of Judas and what that would mean for his eternal destiny. Jesus was troubled that the bold Peter, claiming loyalty, would soon, too soon, deny his master three times. Jesus was not troubled about what would happen to him but what would transpire in the lives of those he loved so deeply. He was deeply troubled because he loved so deeply.

Jesus has many titles: Son of God, Son of Mary, Savior and Redeemer, Good Shepherd. Was one of his titles Trouble-shooter? Through the mystery of the incarnation, Jesus came among us to deal with our big "trouble"—the mystery of sin. In his theological tome *The Glory of the Lord: A Theological Aesthetics*, Hans Urs von Balthasar states, "To have fallen from love is the mystery of original sin." Here is where all our troubles began: to have fallen from love.

Jesus came to locate and eliminate our trouble, our falling from love. Through his death and resurrection, our divine Troubleshooter set us free to turn from sin and embrace the mystery of God's love for us. Reclining next to Jesus was the disciple that Jesus loved so deeply. It was to him that Jesus shared his troubles, his anxiety about what his friend Judas was about to do.

Meditation: In what sense is Jesus a troubleshooter? What is your reaction to the gospel's passage about Jesus being so deeply troubled?

Prayer: Lord Jesus, you worried deeply over the choices of your beloved disciples. You knew the weakness of the human heart and how greed could lead to betrayal, how trepidation could lead to denial. Give us the grace to be faithful; give us the wisdom to make good choices. Send your Spirit into our lives.

The Kitchen Table

Readings: Isa 50:4-9a; Matt 26:14-25

Scripture:
When it was evening,
    he reclined at table with the Twelve.
And while they were eating, he said,
    "Amen, I say to you, one of you will betray me."
        (Matt 26:20-21)

Reflection: Is there any more important place in a home than the kitchen table? It is here that a family gathers not only to be nourished with the fruits of the earth but also to share life experiences day after day. Conversation and communion, talking and eating, be it the family table or the table of the Lord—the center of our lives.

Jesus sat with the Twelve to celebrate the Passover, God's providential liberation of his people. But, as we know, the celebration was marred. Imprisoned by sin, Judas would betray his master for thirty pieces of silver. Table fellowship was violated; the passion of the Lord began to unfold.

In the divine liturgy, just before the celebrant receives Communion, he says inaudibly, "May the receiving of your Body and Blood, Lord Jesus Christ, not bring me to judgment and condemnation, but through your loving mercy be for me protection in mind and body and a healing remedy."

Would that Judas had known and lived that prayer. Would that all of us might be aware of our own capacity to betray our Master.

In the gospels we see Jesus continually at table, be it with tax collectors or sinners or dear friends like Martha and Mary. It was at table that Jesus spoke and listened, ate and drank, laughed and cried. And it was at the Passover table that he left us the great memorial of his life.

Meditation: What meaning does your kitchen table have for you? Who are the people that you invite to sit at your table; who are the people that invite you to sit at their table?

Prayer: Lord Jesus, we give you thanks for inviting us to approach your altar of sacrifice and the table of your Body and Blood. Make us worthy of your presence; help us to be faithful to the call to discipleship. We are weak and sinful. Strengthen us for the journey with your word and sacrament.

On the Night

Readings: Exod 12:1-8, 11-14; 1 Cor 11:23-26; John 13:1-15

Scripture:
I received from the Lord what I also handed on to you,
  that the Lord Jesus, on the night he was handed over,
  took bread, and, after he had given thanks,
  broke it and said, "This is my body that is for you."
    (1 Cor 11:23-24a)

Reflection: In 1971, Loren Eiseley, a paleontologist from the University of Pennsylvania, published an autobiographical work titled *The Night Country*. In this haunting volume, Eiseley describes his encounters with darkness and loneliness. Eiseley knew the night country, the dark side of human existence.

Jesus knew the night country. On the night that he was handed over, many things happened. The Passover meal was celebrated, a meal recalling how God had liberated the Israelites from the land of Egypt; two disciples would betray him, their Master; a mock trial would be held and justice would not be done. Paradoxically, sin and grace came together. The sin of injustice and betrayal met head-on with Jesus' redemptive act of self-sacrifice. What was symbolized at the table was actualized on the cross.

The table and the cross. Our Eucharist is a meal and a sacrifice. The Father's will is that all would be one and that unity be realized in the breaking of bread and in the total self-giving on Calvary. Our challenge is to share both in the breaking of the bread and in the drinking from the cup, the cup of the Lord's passion. Authentic disciples participate in both.

If Loren Eiseley was haunted by darkness and loneliness, we should be haunted by the beautiful passage from the Easter Vigil's *Exsultet*: "O truly necessary sin of Adam, destroyed completely by the Death of Christ! O happy fault that earned so great, so glorious a Redeemer! O truly blessed night, worthy alone to know the time and hour when Christ rose from the underworld!" The night of Holy Thursday and the night of the Easter Vigil are both filled with the light of God's glory.

Meditation: What has been your experience of the night country? What role does the Eucharist play in your spiritual life?

Prayer: Lord Jesus, may we grow in our understanding of the mystery of your sacrificial love. Teach us the art of self-giving; instruct us in the ways of your Father. Too often we fear the darkness of suffering and pain. Too often we turn to self-indulgence and comfort. Strengthen us in our discipleship and our fidelity to your call.

March 29: Friday of the Passion of the Lord
(Good Friday)

Christianity's Uniqueness

Readings: Isa 52:13–53:12; Heb 4:14-16; 5:7-9; John 18:1–19:42

Scripture:
So they took Jesus, and, carrying the cross himself,
    he went out to what is called the Place of the Skull,
    in Hebrew, Golgotha. (John 19:16b-17)

Reflection: In 1981, Fr. Gerald O'Collins wrote *Fundamental Theology*. In this rich text he states that the specific character of Christianity is Good Friday and Easter Sunday, the crucifixion and resurrection of Jesus. It is precisely in the paschal mystery that our identity as disciples of Jesus lies. Through baptism we are all called to participate in the life, death, and resurrection of Jesus.

Good Friday! Suffering and death! The cross! Indeed, for many this day and its events are a stumbling block, an absolute absurdity. But such is not the case for those who see in this mystery God's total self-giving in the person of Jesus. Laying down one's life for the salvation of the world is what redemption is all about. Our hope resides through Jesus' supreme self-sacrifice. Our hope is grounded in the mystery of divine love and mercy.

Love is stronger than death. The wood of the cross blossoms into new life. The chains of sin are broken and the enigma of death is conquered by Jesus' redemptive love. The church cries out, "We proclaim your Death, O Lord, and profess your Resurrection until you come again."

Every world religion has its unique character. The uniqueness of Christianity lies in a specific, particular time: Good Friday and Easter Sunday. In contemplating the cross and the empty tomb we come to believe that our God, who created us, also came to live and die among us, and remains with us still through the gift of the Holy Spirit.

Meditation: What roles do Good Friday and Easter Sunday play in your personal spirituality? How do you participate in the paschal mystery, the life, death, and resurrection of the Lord?

Prayer: Lord Jesus, you teach us how to live and how to die. You teach us how to love and how to have compassion toward all. Draw us more deeply into the mystery of the cross and the mystery of the resurrection. Make us disciples of your way, the way of love and forgiveness.

A Nonsense Story

Readings: Gen 1:1–2:2 or 1:1, 26-31a; Gen 22:1-18 or 22:1-2, 9a, 10-13, 15-18; Exod 14:15–15:1; Isa 54:5-14; Isa 55:1-11; Bar 3:9-15, 32–4:4; Ezek 36:16-17a, 18-28; Rom 6:3-11; Luke 24:1-12

Scripture:
The women were Mary Magdalene, Joanna, and Mary the
    mother of James;
    the others who accompanied them also told this to the
    apostles,
    but their story seemed like nonsense
    and they did not believe them. (Luke 24:10-11)

Reflection: Supreme Court Justice Antonio Scalia spoke at the inauguration of the Thomas More Society in the Diocese of Green Bay back in October of 2010. The Thomas More Society consists of judges, attorneys, and public officials who turn to St. Thomas More as a mentor and model in their work as public servants, a model of integrity and courage.

Judge Scalia mentioned in his address that our culture looks upon believers as "unsophisticated cretins," foolish people who believe in Jesus and the story of his resurrection. It appears that history has not changed. The women in to-day's gospel had a story to tell: Jesus, who was crucified, was alive! The story was taken as nonsense and those who heard it refused to believe.

Thomas More (1478–1535) was a believer who bought the story of Jesus' life, death, and resurrection. So deep was his faith that even the threat of death by beheading did not deter him from following his conscience and maintaining his integrity. Thomas More knew well that if one participated in the Lord's death, one would also participate in his resurrection. More did not live with a divided heart. His faith and his vocation as chancellor of England went hand in hand.

The challenge for all of us, be we public officials or workers in the private sector of society, is to live an integrated faith life. What we profess on Sunday in our liturgy we are to live in the political, social, cultural, and economic sectors of our life. Not to do so, as Judge Scalia would maintain, is to live with a divided heart.

Meditation: What is the connection between your faith and the rest of your life? What happens inside of us when we live with a divided heart?

Prayer: Risen Lord, you gave St. Thomas More the strength to be faithful to your word and true to his conscience. Help us to live with integrity and courage. May we truly believe the story of your love and mercy, in the story of your life, death, and resurrection. Send your Spirit of faith into our hearts and into the entire world.

The Great Divide

Readings: Acts 10:34a, 37-43; Col 3:1-4; John 20:1-9

Scripture:
This man [Jesus] God raised on the third day and granted
    that he be visible,
  not to all the people, but to us,
  the witnesses chosen by God in advance,
  who ate and drank with him after he rose from the
    dead. (Acts 10:40-41)

Reflection: The Easter mystery is the great divide. Do we
stand on the side of life or death? Does death nullify everything
as is the case in Shakespeare's *Macbeth*, where life is that sad
"tale told by an idiot . . . signifying nothing"? Or, is death a
portal leading into the fullness of life, light, and love?

Because of faith in the resurrection of Jesus, we can sing
our faith with assurance:

> To Father, Son, and Spirit blest,
> One only God, we humbly pray:
> Show us the splendor of your light
> In death, the dawn of perfect day.
> (James Quinn, SJ, "O God of Light, the Dawning Day")

In his *Treatise on the Love of God*, St. Francis de Sales uses
the phrase, "the utility of hope." Easter is not only the feast

of faith but it is also the feast of hope. And hope is most "useful," for it gives us the courage to look toward the future with blessed assurance. Jesus is faithful to his word. He has promised to prepare a place for us in the heavenly kingdom and he will come back again to take us into God's mansion. Knowing that a room has been prepared for us gives us the confidence to embrace the trials and tribulations of life.

Elsewhere, Francis de Sales speaks about "this divine germ of immortality." We are infected with a desire to have fullness of life. The apparent finality of death is overwhelming to many of us. We find great consolation in the preface at our funeral liturgy, a prayer that confirms the mystery of the resurrection: "Indeed for your faithful, Lord, life is changed not ended, and, when this earthly dwelling turns to dust, an eternal dwelling is made ready for them in heaven" (Preface I For the Dead).

As Christians, we put all our eggs in one basket, the basket of faith, the basket of the resurrection. This is a divine wager worth making.

Meditation: How do you experience "the divine germ of immortality"? In what sense does hope in the risen life become a graced utility?

Prayer: Loving and gracious God, in raising your Son Jesus from the dead you have given us hope. The mystery of death often overwhelms our spirit. We stand in need of a deeper faith and hope. May the Easter mystery make us agents of your light and love and life. May we truly be your Easter people.

References

February 15: Friday after Ash Wednesday
William James, *Pragmatism* and four other essays from *The Meaning of Truth* (New York: Meridian Books, 1955), 18.

February 25: Monday of the Second Week of Lent
William Shakespeare, *The Merchant of Venice*, IV, i, ll. 198–200.

March 2: Saturday of the Second Week of Lent
Brigid E. Herman, *Creative Prayer* (Brewster, MA: Paraclete Press, 1998), 4.

March 14: Thursday of the Fourth Week of Lent
Jean Sulivan, *Eternity, My Beloved* (St. Paul, MN: River Boat Books, 1998), 80.

March 25: Monday of Holy Week
Michael Himes, *On-Going Incarnation: Johann Adam Mohler and the Beginning of Modern Ecclesiology* (New York: Crossroad, 1997).

March 26: Tuesday of Holy Week
Hans Urs von Balthasar, *The Glory of the Lord: A Theological Aesthetics*, vol. I: Seeing the Form (San Francisco: Ignatius Press, 1982), 214.

March 31: Easter Sunday
James Quinn, SJ, "O God of Light, the Dawning Day," in *Praise for All Seasons: The Hymns of James Quinn, SJ* (Kingston, NY: Selah Publishing, 1994), 79.